Quick & Easy
Avocado Recipes

Contents

About the Book 3
Introduction 4
History & Facts of the Avocado 5
Health Benefits: 6
Recipe #1) Breakfast: Avocado Omlette 7
Recipe #2) Breakfast: Strawberry-Avocado Smoothie 8
Recipe #3) Breakfast: Avocado Breakfast Sandwich 9
Recipe #4) Snack: Easy Guacamole 11
Recipe #5) Snack: Stuffed Avocado 12
Recipe #6) Snack: Avocado-Shrimp Cocktail 13
Recipe #7) Lunch: Avo-Quesadillas 14
Recipe #8) Lunch: Macaroni & Avo 15
Recipe #9) Lunch: Avo-Greens 16
Recipe #10) Snack: Mashed Avocados 17
Recipe #11) Snack: Fried Avocados 18
Recipe #12) Snack: Avo & Cheese Dippers 19
Recipe 13) Dinner: Avo-Kabobs 20
Recipe #14) Dinner: Avocado Soup 21
Recipe #15) Dinner: Avocado Chicken Salad 22
Recipe #16) Dessert: Avocado Fondue 23
Recipe #17) Dessert: Avocado Tea Bread 24
Recipe #18) Dessert: Avo-Pops 25
Closing Thoughts: 26

About the Book

Avocados have seemed to spring into popularity in recent years! No matter what type of food you have, nowadays, avocados are hard to escape from; they are EVERYWHERE. However, most people seem to be stuck in an 'avocado rut', where they often prepare the same types of avocado foods they know and love. Either that, or add a countless number of dollars and cents to try new and exquisite avocado dishes. However, this ALL changes today!

In the pages of this book, you will find a wide variety of quick and easy avocado recipes that you can make from home without breaking the bank! Not only will you find easy to follow and simply delicious recipes, but you will also learn a little about the history and health benefits of this generational "super food"! Let's get started!

Introduction

Before we jump into cutting, cooking, frying and enjoying our avocados, it is time to do a little bit of background work.

We begin this book with a little bit of history and factual information about the avocado. Then, before we cook, we will also learn about the health benefits of avocados and what they are REALLY doing as soon as they enter your body.

Then, it's on to the yummy recipes! We will organize the recipes according to meal, beginning with breakfast; the most important meal of the day. Then, it's on to lunch and finally dinner!

In each recipe, you will be able to find a step-by-step preparation guide along with the all you need to add some avo to your life; what could be BETTER?

By the end of this novel, you too will become and avocado master!

History & Facts of the Avocado

Avocados (also once commonly known as "alligator pears") have a lot of fun facts and history that not many people today are aware of. For one, the avocado is in fact a fruit and not a vegetable! More specifically, it is a member of the berry family due to it's seed and pit.

Another fact that the majority of people do not know is that avocados once possessed a reputation for inducing sexual prowess. Avocados at this time were eaten at risk, as no one wishing to protect their public image from scandalous behavior or slanderous assault. At this time, avocados were NOT high in population AT ALL. In fact, avocado growers had to sponsor public relations campaigns in order for people to cast aside their pre-consumptions about avocados and just enjoy. However, despite this bump in the beginning, we are happy to say that avocados have nothing but a wonderful reputation in today's society!

More tamely, avocados received their name from groups of original Spanish explorers upon discovery in the early 1500's. There are many speculations as to how they decided upon the name "avocado" for the fruit. The probable and most accurate derivative comes somewhere from the Aztec word for fruit ("abucatl") and the Spanish pronunciation of it ("aguacate").

Avocados today are still similar in shape and color as decades and centuries before. Taste often reflects the area of growth, but generally speaking, all generics of the avocado are all within its original characteristics. Avocados currently do and always have grown on trees. This is where they grow and ripen before they are picked. However, in the trees are NOT where the avocado softens. Once the avocado is plucked from the tree, it begins to soften before consumption. In fact, the tree actually can keep the avocado from softening and keep it from going bad for months at a time!

Health Benefits:

AVOCADO NUTRITIONAL INFORMATION:
*based on the average medium avocado
- Calories: 324
- Total fat (g) 30.8
- Carbohydrates (g) 14
- Dietary fiber (g) 10
- Sodium (mg) 0
- Cholesterol (mg) 0

Although high in calorie, the avocado is made up of nutrients and flavors that enhance the natural performance of the human body; therefore, calorie counting should be the least of your worries when eating avocados.

In fact, the avocado can be used to aid in successful weight loss and weight management, due to its many advantages:
- Avocados bring up the body's metabolic rate due to its monounsaturated fats.
- Its high fat content helps the body recognize fullness quicker, reducing overeating.
- The high fat content also reduces temptation on bad foods that are high in sugar or saturated fats.

In terms of daily intake, an avocado is exceedingly rich in its supply of vitamins and minerals, which makes the diet more wholesome and high in aid of overall body health.

Although avocados can be expensive, always try and aim for the organic options. Your body will thank you later.

Overall, an avocado a day can certainly keep the doctor away!

Recipe #1) Breakfast: Avocado Omlette

INGREDIENTS:
*Recipe Serves 1

2 large eggs (or 3 cups egg whites)
1 large avocado
1/3 cup spinach
2 Tablespoons of chopped bell peppers
¼ cup onions
2 tablespoons of butter (healthier option; opt for olive oil)
½ cup of shredded mozzarella cheese

RECIPE GUIDE:
1) Place flat pan on your stove top and turn the heat onto a medium level. Toss in the 2 tablespoons of butter (or olive oil) to coat the pan.
2) In a separate bowl, beat the 2 large eggs (or egg whites) together and add onions, bell peppers and spinach.
3) Pour the egg mix into the pan and allow to cook. Try and keep the omlette flat as it cooks. As soon as it turns a golden yellow (in 3-5 minutes), turn off stove and remove omlette from pan and place onto new plate.
4) In a separate bowl, cut and mash avocado into a spread.
5) Going back to your plate and begin to spread your avocado spread onto the top of your omlette. When finished, fold omlette in half and top with mozzarella cheese and optional seasonings (salt, pepper, paprika, etc.)

ALTERNATE OPTIONS:
- The three vegetables included in the omlette are interchangeable and can be replaced with any other vegetable of your choice.
- Cheese is the same; can be any brand of your choice.
- If you want to spice up your avocado spread, you can throw in optional spices and ingredients as you mash up the avocado.
- You can turn this into a scramble quite easily. Just scramble plain eggs in your pan and add your vegetables last, once scrambled eggs have been almost fully cooked. Instead of an avocado spread, you can simply cube the avocado and add it to your scramble. Top with cheese, as normal.

Recipe #2) Breakfast: Strawberry-Avocado Smoothie

INGREDIENTS:
*Recipe Serves 4

1 large avocado
1 & ½ cups of frozen strawberries
1 & ¼ cups of orange juice (pulp free)
1 cup ice cubes

RECIPE GUIDE:
1) Seed and peel the avocado. Go ahead and half it as well.
2) Place the avocado halves, frozen strawberries and orange juice into the blender and begin to blend on a high level.
3) Add ice cubes accordingly once more and more ingredients have been properly blended.
4) Pulse the blender until all ingredients are properly blended
5) Serve in chilled glasses.

ALTERNATE OPTIONS:
- Although strawberries are preferred, you can switch to any berry of your choice.
- Orange juice can be swapped with pineapple juice if wished, but try not to deviate between the two.
- For a creamier taste, add a dash of milk, almond milk, or coconut water.

Recipe #3) Breakfast: Avocado Breakfast Sandwich

INGREDIENTS:
*Recipe serves 2

3 tablespoons mayonnaise
3 tablespoons plain yogurt
a dash of mustard
1 teaspoon of lemon juice
1 teaspoon of lime juice
Paprika
2 large eggs (or egg whites)
1 Avocado
2 slices of bread (any kind)

RECIPE GUIDE:
1) In a saucepan on a low heat, mix the mayonnaise, yogurt, mustard, lemon and lime juice to create a sauce. Stir to thicken.
2) Cook the 2 large eggs in a separate pan any way you would like (scrambled, over-easy, poached, etc.)
3) When finished, place the eggs onto the bread (slightly toast if desired).
4) Seed and peel the avocado and cut into cubes or thing slices. Then, layer on top of the eggs.
5) Finish by drizzling the warm sauce over the sandwiches. Dash with paprika.

ALTERNATE OPTIONS:
- This recipe calls for sandwich halves, but if desired, you can make each sandwich with 2 pieces of bread (one on top and one on bottom.)
- Any seasonings can be added to the sauce or eggs as desired.
- Opt for nonfat yogurt and light mayonnaise for healthier, lighter options.

Recipe #4) Snack: Easy Guacamole

INGREDIENTS:
*Recipe serves 4

3 avocados
½ cup chopped onions
½ cup diced tomatoes
2 tablespoons of lime juice
3 tablespoons of cilantro (fresh)
1 teaspoon salt
a dash of cayenne pepper or chipotle seasoning (optional)

RECIPE GUIDE:
1) Seed and pit all 3 of the avocados. Cube and mash them into a bowl next.
2) Add in the onions and tomatoes and mix to blend. Continue along with the addition of the cilantro, salt and lime juice.
3) Top with cayenne pepper and serve with desired items.

ALTERNATE OPTIONS:
- You can serve guacamole with chips, tortillas, crackers, or any desired item.
- If you would like, you can mix in a bit of crumbled goat cheese.
- For a more satisfying snack, heat before consumption.

Recipe #5) Snack: Stuffed Avocado

INGREDIENTS:
*Recipe serves 1

1 large avocado
Desired Filling* (see further down for filling options)

RECIPE GUIDE:
1) Seed and pit avocado. Then, slice in half.
2) Fill each half with desired filling.

FILLING COMBINATIONS:
- Cottage Cheese (use 2%)
- Lime Juice & Parmesan Cheese
- Diced Tomatoes & Fresh Onions & Lime Juice
- Poached Egg & Cayenne Pepper
- There is an ENDLESS list!

ALTERNATE OPTIONS:
- Try baking, grilling, or microwaving your avocado when stuffed for a more satisfying and filling snack.
- As this is a snack, try not to add filling combinations that are too high in calorie.

Recipe #6) Snack: Avocado-Shrimp Cocktail

INGREDIENTS:
*Recipe serves 2

1 package serving of frozen shrimp (defrosted)
1 large avocado
1 package of pre-prepared tarter sauce

RECIPE GUIDE:
1) Take your serving of frozen shrimp out of the freezer and lay out to defrost.
2) Seed, pit, and peel your avocado. Then, thinly slice.
3) Arrange your shrimp on small cocktail plates and top with slices of avocado. Drizzle with tarter sauce and enjoy cold.

ALTERNATE OPTIONS:
- You can add seasoning to your desire.
- Tarter sauce is not the only option! You can dip in dill sauce, mayonnaise, or what ever you choose!

Recipe #7) Lunch: Avo-Quesadillas

INGREDIENTS:
*Recipe serves 1

2 large avocados
2 flour or corn tortillas
1 cup of cubed/diced tomatoes
1 cup of cooked Mexican rice
1 cup of refried beans
1 cup of shredded cheddar cheese
1 cup of shredded pepper jack cheese

RECIPE GUIDE:
1) Seed, pit, peal and mash avocados into a spread.
2) Place one tortilla on a plate and spread your avocado spread generously onto it.
3) Top with Mexican rice and beans and sprinkle the tomatoes and both cheese before covering with the other tortilla.
4) Turn on a flat pan on a medium heat and coat with cooking spray (nonstick).
5) Place quesadilla onto pan and wait a minute or so before flipping sides. Be careful to not let anything spill out of the sides or let the quesadilla fall apart.
6) Cut into fours and enjoy.

ALTERNATE OPTIONS:
- Similar to omelets, feel free to get creative and add whatever surprise fillings you desire.
- For a healthier option, opt for black beans instead of refried, and opt for brown rice instead of Mexican rice. Also, opt for non-fat or low-fat cheese.

Recipe #8) Lunch: Macaroni & Avo

INGREDIENTS:
*Recipe serves 1

2 cups of penne pasta
1 large avocado
1 cup of feta cheese
1 cup half & half (or cream of any kind)
sprinkled cinnamon

RECIPE GUIDE:
1) Cook penne pasta in boiled water for 8 minutes or until tender.
2) Seed, pit, peal and mash avocados in a separate bowl.
3) In a saucepan set to a medium to low heat setting, add milk and feta cheese and mix to form a light sauce.
4) Add sauce to avocado bowl and sprinkle lightly with cinnamon. Mix to create sauce.
5) Drain pasta and pour into a separate bowl. Slowly add sauce and stir in evenly.

ALTERNATE OPTIONS:
- Any type of pasta can easily be substituted for penne. For a healthier option, try whole wheat or seven grain pasta.
- Although feta cheese is preferred, you can use any cheese you would like. Try to opt for white cheeses for this light sauce.
- If you desire to add butter, then you may.

Recipe #9) Lunch: Avo-Greens

INGREDIENTS:
*Recipe serves 2

1 bag of pre-prepared salad lettuce (iceburg)
1 large avocado
1 cup of cooked corn
½ cup of tomatoes
1/3 cup of shredded cheddar cheese
¼ cup jalapenos
¼ cup baked tortilla chips
2 tablespoons choice of dressing

RECIPE GUIDE:
1) Throw the shredded, pre-prepared lettuce into a salad bowl.
2) Seed, pit, peel, and cube large avocado and mix into salad.
3) Add the corn and tomatoes and stir in the jalapenos.
4) Mix in dressing of your choice- make sure it is light and not too heavy.
5) Top with tortilla chips and shredded cheese.

ALTERNATE OPTIONS:
- You can mix in and substitute any ingredients of your desire! Try and aim for colorful vegetables to give your salad more life!
- You can easily double or triple this recipe according to the number of guests.

Recipe #10) Snack: Mashed Avocados

INGREDIENTS:
*Recipe serves 1

1 large avocado
Juice of 1 lime
Juice of 1 lemon
¼ cup of crumbled feta cheese
ground black pepper

RECIPE GUIDE:
1) Seed, pit, peel, and cube avocado into a small, single serving bowl.
2) Add juice of one lime and juice of one lemon.
3) Mash ingredients around into a loosely cubed bowl.
4) Sprinkle feta cheese generously around.
5) Heat in microwave for 1 minute to 1 ½ minutes.
6) Top with ground black or red pepper.

ALTERNATE OPTIONS:
- Because this recipe is quite simple, you can spice it up on days you feel you are stuck in your rut. Add meats if you wish.
- Red pepper can be substituted for ground black pepper.

Recipe #11) Snack: Fried Avocados

INGREDIENTS:
*Recipe serves 1

1 large avocado
2 cups bread crumbs
juice of one lime
½ cup shredded parmesan cheese
2 large eggs
2 tablespoons of milk
all purpose flour enough for coating
salt and pepper
frying oil of your choice

RECIPE GUIDE:
1) Seed, pit and peel avocados. Cut into two halves.
2) Coat the avocado in flour.
3) In a separate bowl, mix 2 large eggs (beaten), milk, salt and pepper.
4) Dip the avocado halves into egg mixtures.
5) Coat with bread crumbs.
6) In a frying pan, throw in avocados with an inch of oil
7) Top with parmesan cheese and juice of one lime

ALTERNATE OPTIONS:
- You can use healthier options of frying oil, or you can bake instead for a healthier finish.
- Try to steer away from homemade bread crumbs for this recipe.

Recipe #12) Snack: Avo & Cheese Dippers

INGREDIENTS:
*Recipe serves 1

1 large avocado
½ cup of shredded pepper jack cheese
½ cup of shredded cheddar cheese
1/3 cup of parmesan cheese
juice of one lime
salt and pepper
2 tablespoons heavy cream

RECIPE GUIDE:
1) Seed, pit and peel avocado. Cut into medium to thin dippable slices.
2) In a microwavable safe bowl, mix all cheeses.
3) Mix in heavy cream.
4) Place in microwave and heat until cheese is melted. Take out to stir occasionally.
5) Add the juice of one lime and salt and pepper to taste.
6) Place avocado slices on dippable skewers.

ALTERNATE OPTIONS:
- You can use any cheese type, but try to opt for less of a savory cheese.
- If this recipe makes more cheese than you would like, you can cut the recipe in half.
- Heavy cream can be substituted for healthier options.

Recipe 13) Dinner: Avo-Kabobs

INGREDIENTS:
*Recipe serves 6-8 kabobs

2 large avocados
1 package of grilled shrimp
1 red pepper
1 green pepper
2 onions
1 bottle honey mustard

RECIPE GUIDE:
1) Seed, pit and peel avocados and cube them into larger cubes.
2) In a pan, coat with olive oil and throw in avocado cubes on a low heat.
3) Cut the peppers and onions into slices and add to the pan.
4) Once golden brown, take off heat.
5) Layer the avocado cubes, shrimp, peppers, and onions onto skewers and brush with honey mustard.
6) Place finished skewers on grill for a nice grilled finish.

ALTERNATE OPTIONS:
- Coat with as many seasonings or optional dressings as desired.
- Vegetables are interchangeable.

Recipe #14) Dinner: Avocado Soup

INGREDIENTS:
*Recipe serves 6-8 people

2 large avocados
1 tablespoon of butter
2 onions
1 scallion
1 tablespoon of flour
½ teaspoon of oregano
7 cups of chicken broth
2 cups of milk
1 cup of heavy cream
salt and pepper

RECIPE GUIDE:
1) Seed, pit and peel avocados and cut in halves. Cube the avocado and crush with a fork into a bowl until it is pureed.
2) Melt the butter in a pot and add in onions, scallions, and mix until the onion is clear.
3) Add in flour and oregano and keep mixing.
4) Add avocado puree and mix.
5) Add chicken broth and cook on medium-high for 10 minutes, stirring occasionally.
6) Add milk, heavy cream, salt and pepper, and cook for 5 more minutes on low heat with constant stirring.
7) Serve with remaining thinly sliced avocado on top.

ALTERNATE OPTIONS:
- For healthier options, you can swap the butter, milk, and heavy cream for alternate ingredients.
- Aim for low sodium chicken broth.
- You can top with cheese for an alternate finish.

Recipe #15) Dinner: Avocado Chicken Salad

INGREDIENTS:
*Recipe serves 3

2 large chicken breasts
1 large avocado
½ cup green peas
¼ cup of chopped onions
¼ cup of chopped celery
1 teaspoon coriander
salt and pepper to taste
2 tablespoons of mayonnaise

RECIPE GUIDE:
1) Boil chicken breasts in a small pot with 2 quarts of water until thoroughly cooked.
2) Take chicken out of the pot and let it sit on a cutting board until cool.
3) Using a fork or your hands, shred the chicken.
4) Mix the shredded chick with onions, celery, green peas, and coriander.
5) Seed, pit and peel avocado and mash.
6) Add avocado mash to salad.
7) Mix in mayonnaise.
8) Add salt and pepper to taste.

ALTERNATE OPTIONS:
- You can serve chicken salad on bread, crackers, or eat plain.
- For a more enhanced taste, add lime or lemon juice to taste.
- Mayonnaise can be optional.

Recipe #16) Dessert: Avocado Fondue

INGREDIENTS:
*Recipe serves 1

1 large avocado
1/2 bar of semi sweet chocolate
½ cup of granulated brown sugar
¼ cup regular granulated sugar
Cinnamon
½ cup heavy cream

RECIPE GUIDE:
1) Seed, pit and cut avocado into medium to thin slices.
2) In a pot on a low heat, add chocolate and stir until melted.
3) Add in the heavy cream and both of the sugars.
4) If needed, stir in additional cream or optional additional milk to taste.
5) Sprinkle avocados with cinnamon and sugar.
6) Place avocados on dipping skewers.

ALTERNATIVE OPTIONS:
- Add strawberries and other dippable items to skewers is desired.
- Stir in white chocolate if you would like more of a flavor.
- Top with salt to bring out the sweetness of the dip and of the avocado.

Recipe #17) Dessert: Avocado Tea Bread

INGREDIENTS:
*Recipe makes 2 loaves

light cream cheese* (for spreading)
½ cup organic brown sugar (granulated)
1 tablespoon of pure vanilla extract
¼ cups olive oil (extra virgin)
2/3 cup avocado (pureed)
2 eggs
2 cups zucchini (grated)
½ teaspoon of baking powder
2 cups all-purpose floud
½ teaspoon of baking soda
1 teaspoon of cinnamon
½ teaspoon of salt
¾ teaspoon of all-spice

RECIPE GUIDE:
1) **Preheat oven to 350* F and coat two bread pans (any shape) with olive oil or butter (healthier option being olive oil).**
2) In a separate bowl, combine olive oil, vanilla, sugar and your pureed avocado and mix until the mixture is very smooth- VERY smooth.
3) Add eggs and mix.
4) Add the grated zucchini in a folding-like motion.
5) Sift in the flower, baking soda, baking powder, salt, and spices and mix until evenly blended (be careful of over mixing).
6) Divide mixture and pour evenly into your two pans and place in oven. Cook until top is golden brown (in around 25-35 minutes). BE CAREFUL OF OVER COOKING!
7) Cool and coat with a thin spread of light cream cheese.

ALTERNATE OPTIONS:
- Cream cheese topping is optional.
- Regular sugar can be substituted for brown sugar.
- Maple syrup can be added as a great addition!

Recipe #18) Dessert: Avo-Pops

INGREDIENTS:
*Recipe makes 8 popsicles

1 & ½ cup water (distilled)
2 large avocados
½ cup sugar
½ cup coconut milk (flavored or not)
juice of half a lime

RECIPE GUIDE:
1) Heat a small saucepan and combine the water and sugar to make a sweet, sugar substance. Allow time for cooling before continuation. Sugar should be completely melted.
2) Seed, pit, peel, and slice the avocado in half and blend into a smooth puree.
3) In the blender, add the sugar substance, lime juice, coconut milk, and blend until creamy.
4) Place blended mixture in muffin tins or popsicle molds and place in freezer overnight.

ALTERNATE OPTIONS:
- While unflavored coconut milk is usually the go-to option, feel free to experiment with chocolate and vanilla flavored coconut milks.
- Lime juice can easily be substituted with lemon juice.
- Try making popsicle parfaits by adding a layer of frozen fruit preservatives or chocolate mousse to the bottom of your popsicle tins.

Closing Thoughts:

In this book, you have been presented with a wide variety of quick, simple, and satisfying avocado recipes for any day, any taste, and any time! Hopefully, you have not only gained knowledge about the avocado and it's history through the pages of this recipe book, but that you have also learned the many, many possibilities of avocados in every type of meal- including dessert!

The goal of the reader is to lessen intimidation of both the avocado and of the kitchen, in hopes that the reader will save money and enjoy their healthy, nutrient-enriched lifestyle with their newfound knowledge.

Keep in mind upon finishing that this is just the START to the many possibilities that avocados can offer your food! Try and take the combinations and information that you have learned and create your own recipes! Don't let yourself be stuck in a food rut any more!

Printed in Great Britain
by Amazon.co.uk, Ltd.,
Marston Gate.